# Courage, Blood and Luck

# Courage, Blood and Luck

*Poems of Waterloo*

Harry Turner

'A damned nice thing, the nearest run thing you ever saw in your life.'

Arthur Wellesley, Duke of Wellington

Pen & Sword
**MILITARY**

First published in Great Britain by
### PEN AND SWORD MILITARY
*an imprint of*
Pen and Sword Books Ltd
47 Church Street
Barnsley
South Yorkshire S70 2AS

Copyright © Harry Turner, 2013

ISBN 978 1 78303 014 9

The right of Harry Turner to be identified
as the author of this work has been asserted by him
in accordance with the Copyright, Designs and Patents Act 1988.

A CIP record for this book is available from the British Library.

All rights reserved. No part of this book may be reproduced or transmitted
in any form or by any means, electronic or mechanical including
photocopying, recording or by any information storage and retrieval
system, without permission from the Publisher in writing.

Printed and bound in England by
CPI Group (UK) Ltd, Croydon, CR0 4YY

Typeset in Palatino by CHIC GRAPHICS

*Pen & Sword Books Ltd incorporates the imprints of*
Pen & Sword Archaeology, Atlas, Aviation, Battleground, Discovery,
Family History, History, Maritime, Military, Naval, Politics, Railways,
Select, Social History, Transport, True Crime, and Claymore Press,
Frontline Books, Leo Cooper, Praetorian Press, Remember When,
Seaforth Publishing and Wharncliffe.

*For a complete list of Pen and Sword titles please contact*
Pen and Sword Books Limited
47 Church Street, Barnsley, South Yorkshire, S70 2AS, England
E-mail: enquiries@pen-and-sword.co.uk
Website: www.pen-and-sword.co.uk

# *Contents*

| | |
|---|---|
| Dedication | vi |
| Acknowledgements | vii |
| Introduction | ix |
| The Poems | xiii |

This book is dedicated
to the memory of my wife, Carolyn

# Acknowledgements

The following titles provided the author with the main backbone of research for this book for which he is most grateful.

*Wellington*, Elizabeth Longford, Sutton Publishing, 2001
*The War of the Roses*, Robert Harvey, Constable & Robinson, 2006
*Waterloo Commanders*, Andrew Uffindell, Pen & Sword, 2002
*Wellington in India*, Jac Weller, Greenhill Books, 2000
*Wellington*, Christopher Hibbert, Harper-Collins, 1997
*Waterloo*, David Howarth, Windrush Press, 1968
*Waterloo: The Hundred Days*, David Chandler, Penguin Books, 1980
*Wellington at Waterloo*, Jac Weller, Frontline Books, 1992
*The French Revolution*, William Doyle, Oxford University Press, 2001
*The War with Wellington*, Peter Snow, John Murray, 2010
*Napoleon's Last Gamble*, Andrew Roberts, Harper-Collins, 2005
*Napoleon*, Paul Johnson, Phoenix Books, 2002
*Conversations with Wellington*, The Earl of Stanhope, Prion Books, 1998
*The Hussar General (Blücher)*, Roger Parkinson, Wordsworth Library, 1925
*Waterloo*, Jeremy Black, Icon Books, 2010
*Napoleon & Wellington*, Andrew Roberts, Weidenfeld & Nicolson, 2008
*Wellington's Right Hand*, Joanna Hill, Spellmount, 2011
*Wellington: A Military Life*, Gordon Corrigan, Hambledon and London, 2001
*The Armies of Wellington*, Philip Haythornthwaite, Brockhampton Press, 1994
*The Iron Duke*, Richard Holmes, Harper-Collins, 2002

*Wellington's Charge*, Berwick Coates, Robson Books, 2002
*Voices from the Peninsula*, Ian Fletcher, Greenhill Books, 2001
*Letters from the Peninsula,* Lt. General Sir W. Warre, Spellmount, 1999
*In the Service of the King,* Ian Fletcher, Spellmount, 1997
*Against all Hazards*, Harry Turner, Spellmount, 2001


Thanks also to:

Apsley House, Number One, London (Wellington's house)
The British Museum
The National Army Museum
The Prince Consort's Library, Aldershot

# *Introduction*

The Battle of Waterloo in 1815 was a defining moment for the whole of Europe, possibly the world. It produced a power shift as cataclysmic as the movement of tectonic plates beneath the earth's crust. A hyperbolic judgement perhaps?

Well, consider how the political and social landscape of that great land mass across the Channel would have changed if Napoleon Bonaparte had defeated the allies and continued his relentless expansion. Reflect on how Great Britain would have fared if Napoleon's continental system had flourished, denying us access to markets in Europe and all the attendant social and economic changes that would have followed.

For most of the eighteenth and nineteenth centuries, France was our most consistent enemy: here, in Africa and on the American continent.

Those two 'German' wars in the twentieth century, 1914–18 and 1939–45 were of course significant, but might never have occurred if Napoleon had emerged victorious in 1815.

The Battle of Waterloo is perhaps the most famous of all the great conflicts of the nineteenth century, its name has embedded itself in the English language and people talk unwittingly of 'meeting one's Waterloo'. London's major railway station is named after the battle. A song of that name won the Eurovision song contest and somewhat cheekily, an enterprising company has opened a coffee shop on the station concourse called 'Bonaparte's'.

The battle itself is of endless fascination to historians and politicians and will probably always be so. There have been hundreds of books in several languages about the Battle of Waterloo, analysing tactics and dissecting the political and social background that surrounded the event.

To me, history is a narrative, not just a dry catalogue of dates or even a dreary reproduction of old maps which most people scarcely understand. To recapture the flavour of that great battle, as far as it is possible to do, means visiting and walking on the very ground on which it took place.

I have been privileged to visit the site many times, often in the company of Ian Fletcher, one of our most distinguished battlefield historians. Ian is not an academic, he is an historical enthusiast and that is what makes his trips so exciting.

So people ask, 'So why another book about Waterloo?' My answer is 'Why not?' But dominating this great battle, this vast historical event, for me at least, are three outstanding human personalities:

Arthur Wellesley, the Duke of Wellington
Napoleon Bonaparte, Emperor of France
Gebhard Leberecht von Blücher, Prussian Prince and General.

These three giant figures tower above all others in the narrative, although this is not to diminish the brilliant subordinates from all those countries who took part in the battle.

Let us be clear: I am a Wellington fan. No ifs or buts or qualifications. That said, it must also be stated that Napoleon Bonaparte was a genius. A man who gave his name to an era and who transformed his country in a most extraordinary way.

But Wellington was a winner.
And Napoleon lost.
End of story?
Not quite.

Enter stage left the extraordinary, whiskery, eccentric Blücher of Prussia. At 73 years of age compared to Wellington and Napoleon who were both 45, his intervention at the battle was truly a game-changer. The line between mere eccentricity and raving lunacy is paper-thin. I'm still not sure on which side of it Blücher fell, but he did once believe he was pregnant with an elephant.

So in addition to describing the various set pieces which constituted the battle of Waterloo, I have included brief portraits of these three towering and brilliant historic personalities.

I have chosen to re-tell the story of the Battle of Waterloo in verse because I thought it would be an appropriate way to carry the narrative forward and give it pace.

I am conscious, of course, that I cower in the shadow of Kipling and Tennyson, two giants of literature and poetry whose shoes I am unworthy to polish. But I was inspired as a schoolboy by these two great men, who brought history vividly to life in easy-to-absorb verse.

What does the average person remember, for example, about the Crimean War? OK. That's an easy one. 'The Charge of the Light Brigade', hardly a British triumph.

And Kipling's 'Gunga Din', a poem I cannot read aloud, which I do from time to time, without shedding a tear. So in an age of technological communication, e-mail and Twitter, I offer you, somewhat quixotically, a tale of triumph and tragedy, heroism and failure and I offer it in simple verse.

I am grateful also to three formidable historians who have inspired me with their work and, I am proud to say, their friendship: Patrick Mercer, Ian Fletcher and Andrew Roberts.

Harry Turner<br>
Deepcut, Surrey, 2013

# *The Poems*

| | |
|---|---:|
| 1. The Eve of Waterloo. The Duchess of Richmond's Ball | 1 |
| 2. Napoleon Bonaparte | 7 |
| 3. Arthur Wellesley, Duke of Wellington 1769–1852 | 21 |
| 4. Gebhard Leberecht von Blücher 1742–1819 | 31 |
| 5. Chateau Hougoumont | 43 |
| 6. Hard Pounding | 49 |
| 7. Charge! Charge! Hurrah! | 55 |
| 8. Hold Steady Lads! | 59 |
| 9. Abridged Extracts from the Duke of Wellington's Despatch to Earl Bathurst, Secretary for War | 71 |

# 1

# THE EVE OF WATERLOO
# THE DUCHESS OF RICHMOND'S BALL

## 15 June 1815

Beneath a soaring, vaulted roof
A thousand candles gleam,
It is that fateful, balmy night,
Of Thursday, June fifteen.

Gilt mirrors hang upon the walls,
Each beam of light reflected,
With uniforms of red and green
Exquisitely projected.

Each figure-hugging coat
And richly-polished shoe,
Each tasselled epaulette of gold
And silken sash of blue.

Mix with the swirl of petticoats
And each delicate white shoulder,
As the dainty, satin-slippered feet
With every step grow bolder.

For tonight's a celebration
At the Duchess of Richmond's Ball,
Where no distant hint of conflict
Or no ghostly trumpet call –

Will be allowed to spoil it
Or mar the splendid scene
While the dancers whirl and pirouette
As innocents in a dream.

Is the ball now an example
Of insouciance and pluck,
Of British phlegm as danger lurks,
Of reliance on guts and luck?

It's a great deal more than this it seems,
As earlier in the night,
Wellington himself has heard
He may face a sticky fight.

At Quatre Bras that afternoon
There had been a close-run scrap,
But Prince Bernhard of Saxe-Weimer
Had cleared the crossroads gap.

But in spite of this intelligence,
Wellington will not be moved,
His right place is here in Brussels
As later will be proved.

Though his elegant hawk-like profile
Casts a shadow on the wall,
He displays no hint of nervousness
At history's most famous ball.

And when Lady Charlotte Greville,
A beauty of renown,
Takes his arm to go to supper
In her exquisite satin gown.

He seems relaxed and playful,
Exuding manly charm,
Until the Prince of Orange
Comes close to touch his arm.

'Your Grace will please excuse me,
I have here a dispatch,'
Says the nobleman in a whisper,
The Duke's attention keen to catch.

The music swells and fills the room
With brass and strings combining,
And behind each pretty Chinese fan
Each lady's face is shining.

The young gallants in their scarlet coats
Are still full of dash and daring,
But older officers nearby
Are at the Duke now staring.

Is that a frown across his face?
Has his posture grown uneasy?
Will the Duchess now abort the ball?
As her Grace herself looks queasy.

But she is made of sterner stuff,
Unruffled, cool, phlegmatic,
And she's aware as people stare,
She must do nothing too dramatic.

But the swirl of silk and gleaming pearls
Beneath the chandeliers,
And a brisk quadrille like army drill
Can't mask emerging fears.

The Duke has vanished from the ball,
His supper untouched, cold,
And brother officers too have left,
Both young ones and the old.

But he returns to bid goodbyes
To the Duchess and her friends,
The ball is closed discreetly now
And the celebration ends.

Wellington's all business now,
And asks Richmond for advice,
A fine and detailed map's produced
Of value beyond price.

And Wellington's grim visage
In the guttering candlelight,
Confirms the worst of all his fears
That they just might lose this fight.

'Napoleon has humbugged me,'
Is the Duke's impassioned cry,
'We'll need to fight at Quatre Bras
Under the early morning sky.'

He smoothes the creases on the map,
His aides lean forward too,
'But we'll take Napoleon here,' he says,
Pointing at Waterloo.

# 2

# NAPOLEON BONAPARTE

Once nations trembled at his name
This giant of Belle France,
For he bestrode all Europe,
'Twas if it were entranced.

A warrior and a statesman,
To some a demi-God,
A tactician of great genius
Wielding an iron rod.

No fruit of France's loins was he,
Though he was nobly born,
For Corsica was his birthplace,
An island, rocky and forlorn.

Most persons of ambition
When seeking model roles,
Found him an exemplar and a spur
When pursuing personal goals.

Where even France's traditional foe,
The slow to burn Britannia,
Had secret Bonapartist fans
More than those who loved Espagne.

But Corsica, his island home,
Twice taken by the British,
Was then discarded with a shrug
As ungovernable and skittish.

Ruled earlier by Genoa
For a century or more,
The Italians too, found it troublesome,
A permanent running sore.

They occupied the coastal towns,
And neglected the interior,
Where guerrilla bands roamed freely
Proving insurgents were superior.

At length frustration won the day,
And Genoa seized its chance
To sell the island, all of it,
To avaricious France.

The price obtained? Derisory,
A pathetic paltry bait
Which the Genoese took eagerly
In 1768.

The following year, now part of France,
Young Bonaparte was born,
But no meteorites or falling stars
Were from the heavens torn.

In that same year of sixty-nine
Extraordinary to relate,
The future Duke of Wellington was born,
Coincidence? Or fate?

While still a youth untested,
No beard upon his cheek,
Napoleon had visions
Of the life role he must seek.

Deep in his bones his heritage
Was of a Tuscan knight,
A soldier seeking fortune,
A condottiero keen to fight.

A man who'd sell his sword
To whomsoever paid the price,
Who could turn himself from mercenary
To French patriot in a trice.

Gazetted at the age of nine
Into a military school,
A servant of the Bourbons
And subject to their rule.

In seven years as history tells,
He soon became professional,
Artillery was his chosen arm,
A gunner quite obsessional.

Mathematics and map-reading,
Logistics, transportation,
These disciplines and more besides,
He absorbed while at his station.

He also read extensively,
From Plato and Voltaire,
Biography and science
When he found time to spare.

The English constitution too
He consumed with earnest zest,
Light fiction and romances,
But he loved history best.

And thus his character was formed
In body, mind and spirit,
His vaulting lust for knowledge now
Was clearly without limit.

He espoused no love for Corsica
Now it was part of France,
But she was just a springboard too,
To hasten his advance.

He was an opportunist,
Single-minded and aloof,
And Rousseau's abstract 'notion'
Seemed to him a basic truth.

This 'notion' of the general will
With a strong entrenched elite,
And leadership by chosen few
Not mob-rule from the street.

He watched the Revolution
With sagacity and awe,
Perceiving that he'd profit
From this bloody civil war.

He was rapidly promoted,
Reached the rank of brigadier,
His reputation soaring,
His future bright and clear.

But the leader of the terror
Was Maximilien Robespierre,
A supporter of Napoleon
Whose code was awe and fear.

In the cobbled streets of Paris,
Executions could be seen,
As noble heads were severed
By Madame Guillotine.

The River Seine ran scarlet,
And death was on parade,
Though Robespierre himself soon fell
To the basket and the blade.

But in this mist of blood and smoke,
And butchery revolting,
Napoleon's star was brighter now
Still rising fast, not halting.

However, young Napoleon
In 1794,
Was Robespierre's new protégé,
Thus a septic, running sore.

Then arrested and condemned to death,
Public mood began to falter,
Sick now of chaos in the streets
Of blood and senseless slaughter.

Napoleon was thus released
To a few relieving sighs,
To continue like a rocket
His inexorable rise.

But France was still in turmoil,
Full of fury and of strife,
Seeking liberty, equality,
Fraternity and life.

Beyond the wild convulsions
And images of death,
Of ladies knitting by the scaffold
With no disapproving breath.

The foulest deeds grew commonplace,
And people feared the worst,
As Madame Guillotine's keen blade
Would daily slake her thirst.

Now the ancient regime is over,
The Bastille stormed and taken,
There's a bonfire of all privileges,
All royal rank forsaken.

The gilded pomp of monarchy,
The art of courtly manners,
Are all destroyed by citizens
'Neath revolutionary banners.

But the calendar keeps turning,
And revolution loses pace,
Most of its first objectives now
Achieved and put in place.

Napoleon, who's still youthful
Sees his reputation soar,
In Italy at Rivoli
And in Austria's little war.

The European conflicts
Reveal his soldier's art,
A wise head on young shoulders
Backed by a lion's heart.

The French nation is behind him,
As one of their favourite sons,
The Napoleonic age is on us
Under his blazing guns.

He enters the new century
As first consul, then as king,
A self-appointed emperor
As hosts of angels sing.

'All power to the Emperor,'
May his armies still advance,
May the drums and trumpets play aloud
To the glory of Belle France.

The land mass of the continent
Will now bend to his will,
French influence on life and trade
Across boundaries will spill.

One nation though, Britannia,
Seems loath to bend the knee,
She even beats his navy
In a battle out at sea.

His plan has been to dominate,
Using his naval clout,
By blocking trade with Europe
And starving England out.

Frustrated at Trafalgar,
He busies himself at home,
His finger now in many pies
From Vienna, Berne to Rome.

Then early in the century,
His soldiers march to Spain,
Then Portugal its neighbour
To the usual harsh refrain.

But across the English Channel,
The British stir from sleep,
We have pledged to help the Spanish,
It's a promise we will keep.

The next few years are vital,
In the turning of the tide,
And in thwarting French ambition,
And restoring Europe's pride.

The war in the Peninsula
Rages fierce for full five years,
And climaxes with a French defeat
And Napoleon's angry tears.

All this in spite of generals,
Like Junot and Massena,
He cannot beat the allies
Whose intelligence is keener.

It is a bloody conflict,
Full of cruelty and excesses,
And though the British fight defensively,
They enjoy the most successes.

Defeat now for Napoleon
Leaves a bitter lingering taste,
His enormous proud French army
Laid to devastating waste.

Diminished now as captive,
Sent to Elba with dispatch,
It seems this once great emperor
Has at last now met his match.

Wellington's in Vienna
And there's triumph in the street,
For garlands and hosannas
Are what the victors daily meet.

The politicians gather
Like vultures at the feast,
To carve up all of Europe
From the north to the south-east.

But the Corsican usurper
Is not idle in his chains,
He is plotting, he is planning
To turn losses into gains.

Meanwhile the happy allies,
Celebrate their great success,
But fate is stalking silently
To mock their wild excess.

Yea nemesis approaches
From Elba to Belle France,
In a fleet of sailing barges
In a spearhead of advance.

He's landed in the south of France,
Imperial in manner,
Gathering devotees and soldiers too,
To serve beneath his banner.

The charismatic Corsican,
This colossus of Belle France,
To him they flock in thousands,
Human fuel to his advance.

But now among the allies,
There is many a knitted brow,
Their task, to stop Napoleon,
But the question is, just how?

And yet the Corsican is sure,
His destiny awaits,
As his growing band of acolytes
Swarm from each village gate.

To join with him and take up arms
And cast old Louis down,
This powdered popinjay who wears
A most uneasy crown.

The allies too are restless,
The deal they thought was sorted,
With Napoleon in Elba,
His ambitions all aborted.

To alleviate his wounded pride
And the sting of this defeat,
They said 'Be King of Elba now!'
Hoped that would keep him sweet.

From ruling half the continent
As he pursued his goals,
He was now a puppet ruler
Of just a hundred, thousand souls.

His bitterness and anger,
His memory and his pride,
Propels this proud ex-conqueror
To claim God is on his side.

The man who has replaced him
On France's golden throne,
Is Louis the Eighteenth, no less,
A bloated, greedy drone.

From Antibes on the Cote d'Azur
Through farms and vineyards green,
Napoleon's return now seems
More real than just a dream.

His exile days are over
Where he grew fat and lazy,
And was 'gawked' at by grand tourists
Who thought the Corsican was 'crazy'.

He's now 'Homme Providentiel'
By popular acclaim,
As onwards still he marches,
His old status to reclaim.

Some of his old compatriots
Still royalist, like Massena,
Believe they can upset his plans –
Claim their blades are much keener.

Then just shy of Grenoble,
His caravan is halted
By an infantry battalion,
Charged to see this march aborted.

But the Corsican is on a roll
And he dismounts his steed,
He walks alone before their guns
And begs them 'Do your deed!'

His military band behind him,
The 'Marseillaise' begin to play,
As the Corsican stands proud and cries,
'Will you, your Emperor slay?'

There follows a great silence
And much shuffling of feet,
'You men must surely know that I
Cannot countenance defeat.'

The infantry confronting him
Gives voice to a ringing cry,
'Vive l'Emperor' they sing,
And it reaches to the sky.

Unstoppable, triumphant
He continues on his way,
And one who's come to capture him
Is old comrade Marshal Ney

Who finds it impossible to thwart him,
And he falls upon his knee,
'I pledge my life and cavalry
To my Emperor – to thee.'

In Paris there's confusion
And still many a knitted brow,
The Corsican must be vanquished,
But in God's name now – just how?

At last the waiting's over
And a climax is at hand,
A battle royal is looming,
One both terrible and grand.

The paradox is awesome,
Monumental yet quite true,
As Napoleon now approaches
His own personal Waterloo.

# 3

# ARTHUR WELLESLEY DUKE OF WELLINGTON

# 1769–1852

His birth was not in England
Midst oaks and pastures green,
Nor in bucolic splendour
Or mansions quite serene.

But across the boiling Irish Sea
In the damp old Emerald Isle,
The greatest Englishman of all
Was born in simple style.

In later years, 'tis rumoured,
He stated with some force,
Having a birthplace in a stable
Doesn't make a man a horse.

His mother died when he was twelve,
And the boy was sent to Eton,
Lacklustre though his prowess was,
His spirit was not beaten.

But the general view, a harsh one
That the lad was undistinguished,
Made him quit his school at age fifteen,
Academic life extinguished.

But all, however, was not lost
As he was bundled down to Brighton,
And by the bracing seaside air,
Private tutors had a fight on.

To try to force the lad to learn
Pure mathematics and dull science,
But hopes of scholarship, alas,
Showed scant chance of compliance.

At seventeen the scrawny youth
Was sent to Angers, France,
To study equitation here
And his language skill enhance.

Students of history may note,
'Twas ironic that perchance,
This future English warrior duke,
Learnt his horsemanship in France!

He also became fluent
In the language of his hosts,
This skill would serve him handsomely
In his exalted senior posts.

He took his first commission
On a day he'd long remember,
As lieutenant in the 76th
On Christ's birthday in December.

His star at once began to rise,
And in scarcely sixty days,
He was an aide-de-camp in Ireland –
An accelerating phase.

Within two years of joining
In 1789,
The revolution, out in France
Had sent a shiver down our spine.

This upheaval on the continent,
Its instability and strife,
Marked Wellesley indelibly
And he'd retain it all his life.

His career now as a young gallant
Continued to advance,
He took command of the artillery.
His first action?  Toulon, France.

Now ranked lieutenant-colonel
At the age of twenty-four,
His duties were in Flanders
In yet another 'Frenchie' war.

He learnt much from these skirmishes,
And later, full of years,
He confided in Lord Stanhope
That one of his deepest fears –

Was leading men in conflict
Without adequate supplies,
Or fighting in foul weather
'Neath murky, foreign skies.

The event-packed 1790s
Were drawing to a close,
But from all the nations spread worldwide,
The French were still our foes.

Thus Wellesley now colonel,
Was to command the 33rd
And he sailed with them to India,
Where much later he was heard –

To claim that 'India made him'
And was his turning–point in life,
As indeed he flourished splendidly
In that land of heat and strife.

Two memorable battles
In Mahratta and Mysore,
Enhanced his reputation
As nothing had before.

The greatest threat to British power,
To our jewelled Imperial Crown,
Was naturally Napoleon's France
Who longed to cast us down.

As conquerors and rulers
Of the vast exquisite land,
And they sought to prosecute their aims
By taking by the hand –

Our enemy a noble beast
The Sultan of Mysore,
Well-known as 'Tippoo Tiger'
And red in tooth and claw.

To find allies in this struggle,
We were grateful, even glad,
To fight beside the sepoys
Of the Nizam of Hyderabad.

At length the roguish Tippoo
And his warriors faced defeat,
And in this scrap young Wellesley
Learnt of things he'd not repeat.

Such as fighting after darkness,
When visibility was poor,
But holding men steady
Till the foe was at the door.

He later became famous
For this coolness and élan,
And his tactic of delaying fire
Was now his master plan.

He'd wait until the enemy
Were so close you'd smell their breath,
Then release a rolling volley
Of musket fire and death.

His last big Indian conflict
And some would say his best,
Was the bloody battle of Assaye
Which he fought with skill and zest.

This village on a shimmering plain
With green parrots, swooping kites,
Presented tactically and physically
The most testing of his fights.

To locate and fix the enemy
Required a dangerous river cross,
But his scouts had said 'impossible'
As they'd endure horrendous loss.

But Wellesley decided,
Although the banks were steep,
He'd ride down there himself and check
And look before he'd leap.

On Diomed, his stout young steed,
He trotted to the fore,
And found a spot below the trees
'Quite fordable to be sure'.

He turned and gave a rallying cry
And was first into the river,
The water reached his horse's chest
And its flanks began to quiver.

But following bold Wellesley's lead
As he splashed across the water,
His men and guns slid down the banks
And not one man would falter.

Though outnumbered by the enemy
At odds of six to one,
The British took the village
Under that burning sun.

The Mahrattas French-trained troops
Who entered in the fray,
Were no match for Wellesley's sepoys
Who though bloodied, won the day.

'Tis a fact that's often stated
When reflecting on this strife,
That Wellington said quite clearly,
'Twas the battle of his life.

The bloodshed and the slaughter
Of both men and horses too,
Made Wellington when full of years
Compare Assaye to Waterloo.

He sailed back home to England
A hero and a knight,
After eight long years in India
His future now looked bright.

But snobbery and prejudice
Prevailing at that time
Dubbed him a 'sepoy general' –
- A heinous, social crime.

Early in the century
He overcame this slur
And senior ranks, reluctantly
To his great skills did defer.

Yet the continent of Europe
Was still a cauldron of unrest
With the French plans for expansion
Putting nations to the test.

The stern drumbeat of history
Showed that aggression would succeed
Unless free men were willing
To face down Napoleon's creed.

But Wellington was a wealthy man
Worth fifty thousand pounds
Not quite a nabob some would say
As he performed his social rounds.

During the next few 'bridging years'
His reputation grew
He married Kitty Pakenham
Though she was thought a shrew.

Holy matrimony alas –
Though indelicate to state –
Did not prevent young Wellesley
From flirting like a rake.

His true passion was the army –
'Twas his one and only love –
But he mixed this in with politics,
More a hawk than liberal dove.

Now a Tory member
In a safe Conservative seat
He was appointed Irish Secretary
The synergy complete.

He enjoyed one classic meeting
In London's Downing Street
When he encountered Nelson,
The hero of our Fleet.

Meantime across the Channel
The cauldron still was bubbling
And Napoleon's plans to dominate
Were both arrogant and troubling.

The war in the Peninsula
We hoped may turn the tide
And drive the French from Portugal
With our allies on our side.

With Wellington supremo
And the King's Own German Legion
We clashed in mighty conflicts
Across the huge Iberian region.

Talavera and Rolica
Alcantara and Sobral
Above these battlefields there hung
A most devastating pall.

Albuera and Oporto
Cuidad Rodrigo in the north
Across dusty plains and valleys
Our soldiers proved their worth.

At Badajoz we breached the walls
Of a fortress monumental
And Wellington was seen to weep
A rare moment sentimental.

At length from five years' fighting
When the French had slunk away,
With Napoleon's men most roundly trounced
We claimed we'd won the day.

But the Corsican usurper
Was not easily suborned
And the British and their allies
Should have surely all been warned –

That he would slip his fetters
Gather men and weapons too
And give us one last battle
On the field of Waterloo.

# 4

# GEBHARD LEBERECHT VON BLÜCHER

## 1742–1819

The village of Gross Renzow
Close to Rostok by the sea
Has a view across the Baltic
With Sweden in its lee.

'Twas in this Prussian fishing port
That Blücher first drew breath
And would confound, amaze and shock all men
Through life until his death.

One of nine brothers born here
He was a lusty, healthy child,
Not academic in the least
But inquisitive and wild.

The family's wish for their dear son
Was a life of rural bliss
Where he could be a farmer
And receive fair nature's kiss.

But already in the young man's veins
Ran the hot blood of a soldier
And whilst still in his teenage years
He sought a life much bolder.

First a Swedish soldier
In those hectic early years
He actually faced the Prussians,
Confirming family fears –

That he was a mere mercenary,
A youth who loved to fight
Under any country's banner
From night to dawn's first light.

Proud Prussia in those early years
Was stirring with ambition,
Part of a clutch of minor states
All seething with sedition.

When Blücher, still a subaltern
In the service of the Swedes,
Was captured by the Prussians
They fulfilled his deepest needs.

A fur-lined cloak and uniform,
A hussar's boots and sword,
His allegiance switched immediately
Upon his solemn word –

To serve the Prussian nation
And see it reach its goal,
To fuse the disparate Slavic states
With Prussia as its soul.

He rose like Mercury through the ranks
Battle-hardened and heroic,
His love for drink and sex and life
Scarcely marked him as a stoic.

Charismatic and eccentric,
Untutored, brash and rude,
His soldiers loved him dearly
Though his style was rough and crude.

He dubbed his men his 'children'
As he led them into battle,
They called him 'Father' in return
And would follow till death's rattle.

In a mighty spat with Prussia
And its enormous Russian neighbour
Mad Blücher could be seen upfront
While brandishing a sabre.

His methods were unorthodox
Lacking subtlety and style,
He was quite ruthless with the enemy
Showing cruelty not guile.

And thus, still in his thirties
Promotion passed him by
And in anger and frustration
'Bad boy' Blücher's savage cry –

Was 'To hell with you, I'm leaving,
For promotion I'll not wait.'
He wrote an angry letter too –
To King Frederick the Great.

His life now changed dramatically,
He abandoned spurs and sword
And turned again towards the land
To become a rural lord.

But a farmer's life, he quickly found
With rich good earth to till
Was no match for the cannon's roar
And the surge of battle's thrill.

But fourteen years were due to pass
Before he took up arms,
He fathered seven children
And enjoyed domestic charms.

But all around in Europe
Were volcanic insurrections
Where nation states now sought to change
Their political directions.

Still stirring in his lion's heart
And pounding in his brain
Was the call to arms, to conflict
To the war drum's keen refrain.

King Frederick of Prussia died
To be succeeded by his son.
At this news Blücher kissed his wife
And reached up for his gun.

The new young king liked Blücher
And at once gave his permission
For Blücher to retain the troops
And reinstated his commission.

He buckled on his sword and spurs,
His helmet burnished bright,
This warrior of Prussia now
Was spoiling for a fight.

Turmoil throughout Europe
And in revolutionary France
Gave Blücher most fortuitously
A second golden chance.

To skirmish with Napoleon's men
As a colonel of hussars
In Austria and Holland
The Netherlands and Maas.

From the outbreak of the war with France
In 1792
Blücher saw action countless times
And his reputation grew.

Promoted major-general,
His energy prolific,
He continued to exhort his men
With instructions quite specific –

To always face the enemy
Those hated sons of France
'Go forward all my children,
Attack with sword and lance.'

In those lulls between the fighting
When lesser men would rest,
He hunted and he partied
With superhuman zest.

His drinking was prodigious,
His behaviour quite appalling.
He gambled and combined it all
With his noble soldier's calling.

For a fellow in his fifties
With an unslaked lust for life,
His colleagues often wondered
If he simply sought out strife.

But this crazy, giddy roundabout
Was destined soon to cease
When Prussia sought neutrality
And finally made peace.

Hot-blooded Blücher hated this
As he longed to fight the French,
Thus being told 'You're neutral now'
Was a devastating wrench.

But eleven years were now to pass
And he took on peacetime roles,
But none of these, though worthy
Were remotely like the goals –

He'd set out as a warrior
And Prussia's proudest son,
He didn't wish to wield a pen
And much preferred the gun.

Then early in the century
As the French Empire still grew
Blücher begged King Frederick to act
And neutrality eschew.

But the French success at Austerlitz
Sent out a clear stark warning
That Prussia was withering on the vine
And a cold harsh day was dawning.

Meantime in the Peninsula
Through Portugal and Spain
The French now swarmed in thousands
Yet more territory to gain.

At last back in the thick of it
Blücher's mood was quite ecstatic,
He'd face the French a dozen times
Some encounters quite dramatic.

He was even briefly captured
After a bloody battle,
His sweating horse shot under him
Where he heard the beast's death-rattle.

Extraordinary though it is to tell
He had a meeting face-to-face
With Napoleon Bonaparte no less
Who greeted him with grace.

'You are a Prussian hero'
Said the emperor with a smile,
'I admire your sterling qualities,
Your ferocity and your guile.'

'Do tell your King, however,
That he should sue for peace,
We have no wish to fight with you,
May hostilities now cease.'

Blücher, now a general
Was released in an exchange
With a Frenchman of a similar rank,
Now this was passing strange.

Thus at Tilsit in the summer
A peace was duly signed
Leaving Prussia weak and powerless
As Napoleon had designed.

This once great Slavic country
Was now carved up like a joint
From Elba and its territory
To its farthest western point.

His mental state confused now
And subject to fits of rage
Poor Blücher the warrior
Was like an animal uncaged.

He wallowed in excesses
Fornicated like a goat,
His dreams were psychedelic
Madness had him by the throat.

Once with a rambling anecdote
And rumbustious drinking binge
He demonstrated he had crossed
The lip of hell's mad fringe.

'I'm pregnant with an elephant,'
Was the crazed hussar's wild cry
But no man tried to calm him –
Indeed no man dared try.

But nine years in the century
The Austrian nation stirred,
Declared war on Napoleon's France
Their loyalties now blurred.

Blücher pleaded with King Frederick
'Let Prussia take up arms'
To throttle all Napoleon's plans
And ignore his subtle charms.

'Twas not to be, however,
And Frederick refused,
He hoped by staying neutral
The war would be defused.

Blücher though, inevitably
Still itched to grasp the sword
He fulminated uselessly –
As an impotent war lord.

But when news reached the Prussian's ears
Of the fierce Peninsular War
And a hero, name of Wellington,
The news touched Blücher's core.

At last the Prussians stirred from sleep
To declare war on the French
By joining with the Russian Tsar,
Though for Frederick 'twas a wrench.

The allies led by Wellington
Now drove the French from Spain,
Brave Portugal was free again
Though they'd suffered grievous pain.

Napoleon's army soundly thrashed,
The Emperor unseated,
The first time in a dozen years
The Juggernaut defeated.

But Blücher too took credit
For Napoleon's defeat,
Having battled with the French for years
Victory tasted very sweet.

Now a venerable man of seventy
Twice wounded, often ill,
There is no conflict he would shun
Nor avoid each battle's thrill.

With Napoleon in Elba
His charisma much reduced
It was by Wellington's stern qualities
That Blücher was seduced.

The Peninsular War was finished,
Iberia was free,
Wellington was in Vienna
To plant a victory tree.

But Napoleon defeated
Still found it in his heart
To pay tribute to old Blücher
And praise the Prussian's art –

As a warrior and leader
Who could not concede defeat
Who would always come in fury
Every obstacle to meet.

Some others said that Blücher
Was clearly an immortal
Whose spirit would not lose its fire
And pass through heaven's portal.

In June he sailed to England,
Was greeted with applause,
But in his savage warrior's heart
He knew peace was just a pause.

He dined with dukes and princes
Was a boisterous party guest,
Met Wellington, who he admired
And shook his hand with zest.

Yet he felt deep in his Prussian bones
The smallest ache of doubt,
Had the allies been too lenient
Now the French were down and out?

Was the congress of Vienna
A mere worthless settlement?
He told all who would listen
Of his raging discontent.

But his spirits soon revived again
When fresh news reached his ears
Of Napoleon's escape from Elba
Which fuelled the allies' fears.

'But this is the finest stroke of fate,'
Cried Blücher, now ecstatic,
'We can whip the French again – this time
And let the finish be dramatic!'

And so it was, as history shows
Blücher's prophecy was true,
They'd fight the French just one more time
Near the village of Waterloo.

# 5

# CHATEAU HOUGOUMONT

Beneath an ancient twisted elm
And a scowling leaden sky,
Sat Wellington upon his horse
His spyglass to his eye.

Just off centre to his right
Encircled by high walls
Stood a pitch-roofed noble chateau
That echoed with sharp calls –

Of the sergeants of the foot guards
Who were invested in this place
To hold it 'gainst all comers
On firm orders from His Grace.

The chateau, name of Hougoumont
Was vital to the battle,
The French must never take it
They'd be fought to death's last rattle.

The earth around the chateau
Was sucking wet with mud
Thus cannonballs fired by the French
Simply landed with a thud.

The French assaults on Hougoumont
Began with fiery zest
As Napoleon knew with certainty
That from the allies he must wrest –

This crucial prize from Wellington
If he was to win the day
So cannon, gun and bayonet
Were hurled into the fray.

At nine o'clock, still full of pep
Astride his huge white horse
Napoleon was keen to fight
And force the battle's course.

His heavy guns poured fire and lead
Onto the chateau's walls
Accompanied by the piercing sound
Of a hundred trumpet calls.

As cannon fire intensified –
Alongside – in the trees –
A Prussian soldier quite alone
Was discovered on his knees.

Seized by the French and questioned
He then revealed by chance
That he was a lone spearhead
For Blücher's main advance.

Even armed with this intelligence
The French did not take heed,
Instead of redeploying
Their attack increased in speed.

Historians would later say
As they scrutinised the map
That Napoleon's decision then
Had encased him in a trap.

He'd have to fight upon the ground
That Wellington had picked,
Others would say upon the day
The Corsican was tricked.

Inside the chateau's sturdy walls
Behind its massive gate
The guards and Hanoverians
Took the Frenchmen's full fierce weight.

Meanwhile outside more skirmishes
Which caused the French despair
As waves of frontal charges now
Couldn't break the British square.

But the French had now determined
'Twas the chateau they must take,
Twelve thousand pounding Frenchmen
Made the earth around it shake.

The fighting was ferocious
But the allies still resisted
As dancing flames soared from the roof
And the frenzied French persisted.

With musket-barrels burning hot
That scald each soldier's hand
And veils of smoke that blind and choke
As the guardsmen firmly stand.

But when a moment of dismay
Outside the chateau gate
As a giant Frenchman with an axe
Attempts to penetrate –

Ye gods he's through, with others too
They're all inside the gate,
They stab and hack but are held back
And soon they meet their fate.

The slaughter is forensic
In that scenario of death
The whole detachment is cut down
Save one who still draws breath.

He's just a boy, a juvenile
Of scarcely fourteen summers
No fighting cock like all the rest
But just a young French drummer.

Yet there's more Frenchies at the gate
Struggling to squeeze inside
But stout red-coated British lads
Are there to stem the tide.

The French pour men into the fray
They mass and charge the gate
They push and strain – a human chain
But entry cannot wait –

They know for sure, once past that door
With their superior numbers
They'll overwhelm the allied troops,
Dispatch them to death's slumbers.

Thus crucially the battle's hinge,
The decider of their fate
Will turn upon those British lads
And their closing of the gate.

All day the fighting ebbs and flows
A human lava tide,
French corpses clog the chateau grounds
With several more inside.

But the brave Redcoats at Hougoumont
Stand shoulder next to shoulder
Through cannon's thud and comrades' blood
As each French assault grows bolder.

For a full eight hours 'tis hell on earth
But the British still hold fast
They will never give the chateau up
Till each man has breathed his last.

Elsewhere, beyond old Hougoumont's walls
There is other fighting too,
With cavalry and cannon fire
Mixed in a devil's brew.

# 6

# HARD POUNDING

Napoleon has grown excited
For the left of the allies is weak
And the cannonade he has provided
Is the soft spot his big guns now seek.

But alas for the French he's mistaken,
He's pursuing a wild forlorn hope
Because Wellington's men are positioned
On the hidden reverse of the slope.

All morning the battle still rages,
Ebbs and flows like a fiery tide
And many a youth in both armies
Is obliged to take death as his bride.

Past noon in the east, midst thick woodland
More black-coated figures appear,
They are Prussians, not Frenchmen, advancing
Led by von Bülow, a man without fear.

Napoleon senses the danger
He must launch a massive attack
For time now is short – of the essence
If the French are to claw anything back.

French Marshal d'Erlon is given the task
Of mounting a monstrous assault
A quarter no less, of the army,
If he fails, he's aware it's his fault.

The ground is uneven and broken
With scant cover for all the French troops
But in mass they surge forth, sweeping in from the north
All shoulder to shoulder in groups.

The first wave has tasted success
As La Haye Sainte falls to Belle France
But briefly it seems, and Napoleon's dreams
Seem unlikely just now to advance.

Those lads of the King's German Legion
Have fought with most noteworthy zest
They have faced off attacks, with dense woods at their backs
And survived the most terrible test.

And in this swirl of mud and blood
Of musket fire and slaughter
One British officer's clear call
Is 'Give the French no quarter.'

Young men, both French and English
With beardless, smooth white cheeks
Attack, withdraw, are stopped or slain
As each his glory seeks.

As acrid smoke curls like a snake
And hovers o'er the fray
The crack of guns and the whine of shot
Now punctuate the day.

The horses too are casualties
As neighing they're cut down,
Intestines spilling in the mud
And in their blood they drown.

With telescope held to his eye
Wellington views the scene,
He's picked his ground most carefully
And his mood seems quite serene.

But in his heart he knows for sure
That Hougoumont is the key
And La Haye Sainte and all the rest
Must be secured and now set free.

The French are pressing strongly
They've thousands in the field
They stab and cut and shoot and slash
Surely their foes must yield?

Years hence historians argue
About tactics on this day
How d'Erlon's troops massed in columns
As they surged into the fray.

Whereas 'tis said, quite sagely
That the allies' thin red line
Was the superior tactic
And was operationally fine.

The orchard and the garden
Of the iconic La Haye Sainte
Are raked by furious gunfire
But resistance there is faint.

Good fortune though smiles down on us
And the building does not burn
And the gallant German Legion
Further honours now will earn.

Both cut and thrust and ebb and flow
And the deadly thud of lead
As cannonballs –those spheres from hell –
Add to the growing dead.

Some men, now quite exhausted,
Stagger and fall unhurt
Their uniforms a ragged mess
As their faces plough the dirt.

An officer, a Frenchman,
A youth scarce out of school
Is cut in two by a cannonball,
Is he a hero? Or a fool?

On a gentle hill, above the fray
Astride a fine white horse
Napoleon Bonaparte surveys –
The raging battle's course.

His trusted aide and confidante
One de la Bédoyère
Leans close to whisper naked facts
Into his emperor's ear.

If the French can't drive a wedge now
Twixt Wellington and his aides
And thus divide the allied team
The prospect of victory fades.

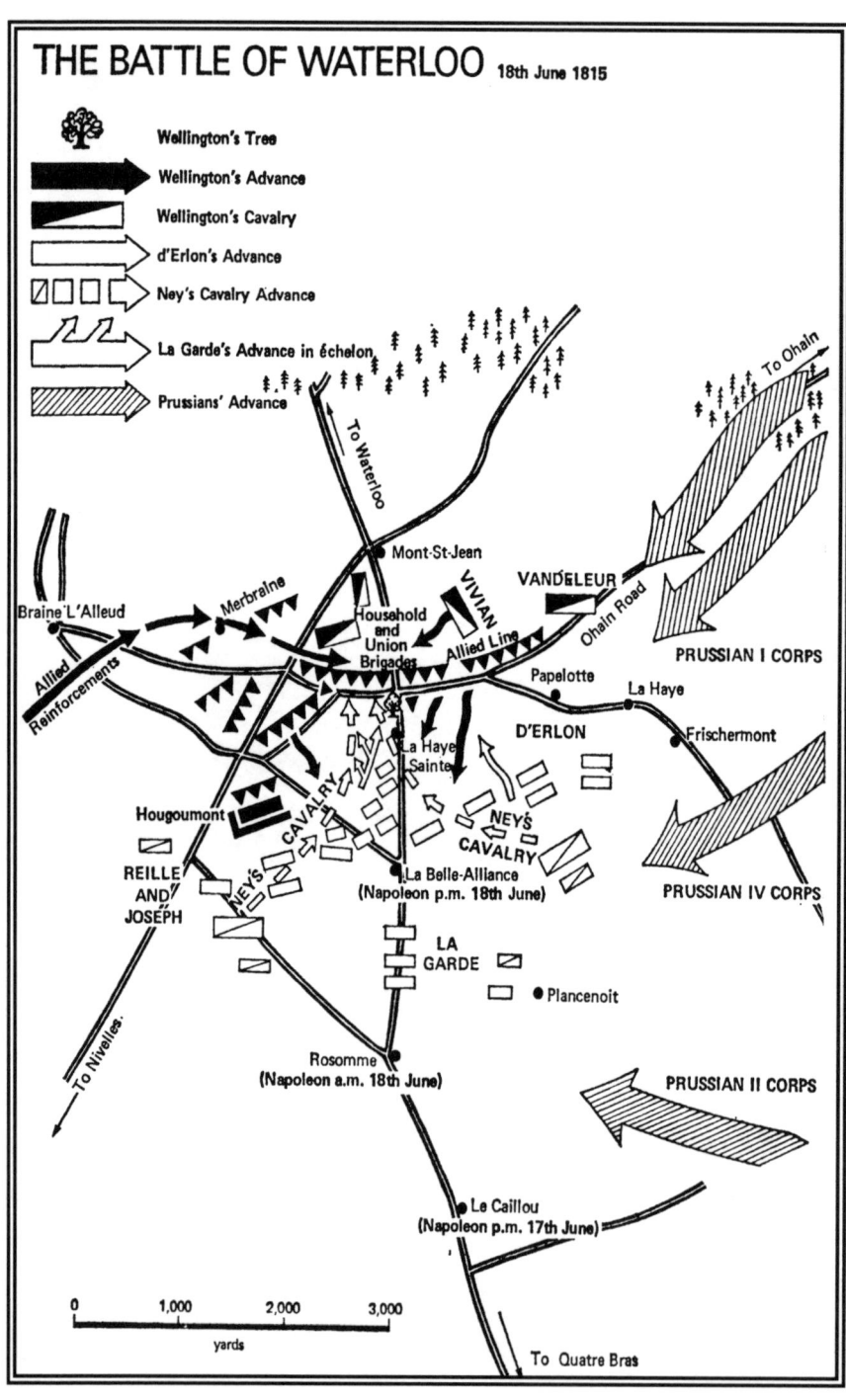

# 7

# CHARGE! CHARGE! HURRAH!

The losses now on either side
Of the wounded and the dead
Have slowed the rhythm of the fight
As the churned earth's now turned red.

Desperate commanders
On both sides of the battle
Are grasping any chance now
To defer grim death's last rattle.

The French will mount a fierce attack
With a gallant cavalry charge
But without supporting men on foot
This error will loom large.

'Tis thought that 'twas Napoleon
Who ordered Marshal Ney –
'A thousand horses in the charge –
It is the only way.'

But later he denies it
Says Ney was just a fool
And Ney is later put to death
Cast down, a broken tool.

On the English side there's tragedy
As d'Erlon's soldiers mass
To launch a fierce French attack
On Picton's men – alas!

The general has ordered 'bayonets fixed'
To face the hail of lead
Outnumbered by the Frenchies, though,
He's shot clean through the head.

A little later in the fight
Our cavalry come to the fore
A seldom-used attaching tool
In this most bloody war.

Scot's Greys and Inniskillings
Royal Horse Guards and the rest
Surge forth with jangling harnesses
To put Frenchmen to the test.

The pounding hooves beat a tattoo
With the swish of fresh-drawn swords
And those giant English horses now
Defy descriptive words.

The French are all sent reeling
Under this grand assault
And those who escape the lance and gun
Are quickly trapped and caught.

# 8

# HOLD STEADY LADS!

The ammunition's running low
In the farmhouse La Haye Sainte
And thus defensive firing now –
Is dangerously faint.

'Shot and powder' is the plea
From the hard-pressed allied troops
As they now keep the French at bay
Through the wall's small firing loops.

By six o'clock the KLG –
The famous German Legion
Are desperately still holding on
Proud heroes of their region.

But as the combat rages on
With every inch of ground
Disputed in this deadly fight
We hear an awful sound.

'The French are in!' goes up the cry
As the allied line collapses
And French in hundreds swarm inside,
To exploit the allies' lapses.

A sergeant of the cavalry
From the famous 'Royal Scots Greys'
Seizes a French Gold Standard
For which he earns high praise.

His name is Sergeant Ewart,
A man of pluck and guts
Who snatched the French Gold Eagle
And survived a dozen cuts.

But sad to say, the cavalry charge
Though majestic to observe,
Has gone a league or so too far
For tactically to serve.

French retribution follows
In a merciless assault,
A third at least of all our men
Are slaughtered, cut or caught.

At four o'clock on that same day
As the battle looms ferocious
The killing is like butchery
And the men's wounds are atrocious.

But Napoleon knows, none more than he,
To avoid defeat's sour taint
He must capture that walled stronghold
Known as the farmhouse, La Haye Sainte.

La Haye Sainte is a talisman,
A key point in the strife
A golden star – so near yet far
Costing much in blood and life.

Across the smoking battlefield
Mad chaos everywhere,
The allied tactic in defence
Is the famous British square.

Eighty French squadrons, awesomely
Are deployed against each square
But though rebuffed they still ride on
To local officers' despair.

Napoleon, it seems to them
Has found it strangely hard
To mobilise his best crack troops –
The great Imperial Guard.

There is a joke among the French
That causes the grimmest chortle,
The Imperial Guard are <u>never</u> used
Hence they are dubbed immortal!

This is the moment some will say
Most crucial of the day
When a strongpoint like the farmhouse
Could soon the battle sway.

The French have won advantage,
Can they penetrate our line?
Can they punch a hole in our sturdy lads?
Will we deploy in time?

Several blasts from their artillery
And a deadly hail of lead
Cuts through the Inniskillings,
Many wounded, still more dead.

A pivotal moment then it seems
In this most bloody fight,
If Blücher does not soon arrive
Wellington will pray for night!

The Duke is highly visible
As he rides along the line
His profile like an eagle,
His presence quite sublime.

Another place – named Plancenoit –
Sees fighting most severe,
Indeed as fierce as Hougoumont
And indubitably clear –

That if the French reclaim it
'Twill be a vital hinge
And to lose it for the allies
Will make British generals cringe.

Count Bülow, on the British side
Is driven from this place,
Pulverised by French assaults
He's sure now to lose face.

It's Napoleon's intention
To divide the allied ranks
To cut them up like a Sunday joint
And carve the redcoats' flanks.

But in the trees, not far away
The Prussians are approaching
As half-a-league, by half-a-league
On the battle they're encroaching.

Amidst the smoke and violence
The roaring and the screaming
There still exists humanity –
With men capable of dreaming.

Exhaustion like some noxious plague
And rest a distant hope,
Oh men should sleep, profound and deep
And husband strength to cope.

For those who hoot with the owls at night
With their broadswords still undrawn
Will not, at the rising of the sun
Fly with eagles at first dawn.

For young men still in tender years
As they crouch in stinking mud
And hear the cries of dying friends
And taste their own sour blood –

Do some still dream of childhood?
Of a loving mother's care?
Do they wince now at the sound of shot
As at death's foul face they stare?

Yes dreams of home, of sanctuary,
Of simple, gentle pleasures
All locked away on this gross day
Like closely-guarded treasures.

Meantime through fields and woods and streams
The Prussians are approaching
With Blücher and his merry men
On the battle scene encroaching.

The Prussian marshal, bristling
With pride and bloodlust too,
He was unhorsed at Ligny
But sheer courage saw him through.

Magnificent, ridiculous –
A hero, yet a clown,
In spite of being seventy-three
He still seeks a victor's crown.

Napoleon's close lieutenants now
All plumed and shiny-booted
Offer their emperor advice
As in tactics they're all rooted.

They know full well, though war is hell
They've made a vital pledge
To hurl a mass of men and steel
And 'twixt the allies drive a wedge.

Some of his marshals, nervously
Who dare not even ask
Why the Imperial Guard is still unused –
Could they finish off this task?

Were the jaws of the Anglo-Prussian trap
Now closing on the French?
For Napoleon's men was there no escape
Though they squirm and twist and wrench?

But Napoleon is a gambler
And the fight is not yet over
With many a blow received and struck
Before either side rests in clover.

All he seeks is a crack in the line
A chance to play his ace,
A fumble or a weakness
To produce his 'coup de grâce'.

He orders de la Bédoyère
To spread a lie most deft,
That Marshal de la Grouchy's men,
Are close to the allies' left.

Encouraged by mendacity
And clutching now at straws
The Imperial Guard of infantry
Who earlier would pause –

Now advance on Chateau Hougoumont
To press home a last attack,
They all believe misguidedly
That Wellington will crack.

And so to the blare of trumpets
With the Tricolore still flying
The Imperial Guard move forward,
No man afraid of dying.

To the stirring notes of drum and fife
In this last great French attack,
Sublime and unsurpassed in style
There's now no turning back.

Napoleon rides proudly at their head
From the Belle Alliance farm.
Is he invincible, this man?
Will he never come to harm?

But the slope they mount in this grand assault
In the dark, smoke-ladene air
Is soon to change the Frenchies' mood
From triumph to despair.

To meet this wall of human flesh
Are thirty British guns
And Dutchmen and brave Belgians,
Britain's unofficial sons.

The war cries of the French chasseurs
Rise high above the din
And shot and shell, the rain of hell
As the Frenchies now close in.

'Tis then amidst the fire and smoke
With the English troops all steady
Responding to the Duke's clear call
And his order 'Up Guards, ready'.

And surging on the battlefield
The Prussians too advancing,
Their arrival most propitious now
And the allied line enhancing.

Thus Wellington, astride his horse
Snaps shut his telescope,
He senses now that this must be
Confirmation of his hope –

That the Imperial Guard is broken
They're pummelled, stabbed and shot,
The allies are aggressors now
Their soldiers keen and hot.

The ground on which the battle's fought
Is churned into a mire
And broken bodies scattered there
Are enrobed in smoke and fire.

At length with shadows lengthening
On this mutilated ground
And dark clouds threatening menace
There comes a chilling sound.

'La Garde recule!' an awesome cry
That rips keen through the sky
Then 'Sauve qui peut!' replaces it
As brave men fall and die.

It's eight o'clock and darkening
Under the brooding cloud
And now we hear more voices,
Some whispering, some loud.

And then a sight horrendous
Unprecedented too,
The French army is collapsing
They'll never now break through.

Rising up from in a cornfield
The British Guards loom large,
They know they have advantage
As towards the French they charge.

With hearty cries 'Hurrah, Hurrah'
The Foot Guards move as one
With bayonets fixed and eyes agleam
Under the fading sun.

No quarter now is offered
No Frenchman spared the blade,
With lunge and thrust, in God we trust
To see our past debts paid.

The French lines are now ragged
All sense of order trashed
As grenadiers and other guards
Into their flanks are smashed.

To add to this confusion
As the French begin retreating
The Prussian cavalry emerge
To a drummer's warlike beating.

They lance and hack with fury,
No mercy do they show
As they cut down the Frenchmen
Or stun them with a blow.

As the tangled mass still ebbs and flows
Midst many a soldier's shout
'Tis clear to all that now, the fight
Is turning to a rout.

Napoleon is desperate
And seeks a forlorn thrust
With his First Chasseurs and others,
Loyal fighters he can trust.

His generals Christiani and Roguet
Form squares in a fevered attempt
To face down attacks at their sides and their backs
As from cavalry – squares are exempt.

But though squares will often stop horses
Their weakness is simply just this,
They'll be pulverised by grapeshot
Such firepower isn't likely to miss.

The fusillade continues
Relentless and severe
And to some eagle British eyes
They now detect raw fear.

The punishment is awesome
As the British force the pace
The French guards stumble backwards –
'Twill cause a loss of face.

As the British troops move forward
Scenting triumph in the air
They see among the Frenchies
A wave of panic and despair.

Étienne Cambronne their proud general
Is asked now to surrender –
To lay down arms and quit the field
And his sword he now must tender.

Historians of various stripes
Claim many there had heard
Proud Cambronne's angry answer
Which was simply this, just 'Merde!'

But truth to tell, and war is hell
The battered French are fleeing,
A ragged mob, demoralised
Is really what we're seeing.

But the Prussians now take up the chase
To seize each moment's chance,
To butcher Frenchmen ruthlessly
With sword and gun and lance.

Defeated and in disarray
The battle's clearly over,
Napoleon's men have fled the field
Their dead now pushing clover.

At nine o'clock on that same day
By the Belle Alliance Inn
The two victorious generals meet
On Blücher's face, a grin.

He takes the hand of Wellington
As around them soldiers stare
And to a rising tide of cheers
His words are 'Quelle Affaire!'

# 9

# ABRIDGED EXTRACTS FROM THE DUKE OF WELLINGTON'S DESPATCH TO EARL BATHURST, SECRETARY FOR WAR

'At about ten o'clock Napoleon
commenced a furious attack on Hougoumont.
I am happy to add, that it was maintained
throughout the day with the utmost gallantry
by our brave troops'

'It gives me the greatest satisfaction
to assure your Lordship that the army
never on any occasion conducted itself better'

'I should not do justice to my feelings or
to Marshal Blücher and the Prussian army if
I do not attribute the successful result of
this arduous day to the cordial and timely
assistance I received from them'

'I send with this despatch, two eagles
taken by troops in action which
Major Percy will have the honour to lay at
the feet of His Majesty.

'I beg leave to recommend him to your Lordship's protection.

I have the honour to remain etc.'

WELLINGTON